AF606169

Strange Gravity

CEW.

STRANGE GRAVITY

Songs Physical and Metaphysical
by

PAUL PETRIE

Drawings by

CHARLES E. WADSWORTH

THE TIDAL PRESS

1984

ACKNOWLEDGMENTS

Some of these poems have appeared earlier as follows: "The Death Of Birds" in *Yankee*, November, 1980; "The Pause" in *The Atlantic Monthly*, May, 1978; "Bell Song," "Song In The Face Of Endings," "Song Of The Two Ways," "The Widow's Night Song," "After Finding A Spider Building A Nest In Her Hair" and "Summer" in *Time Songs*, Biscuit City Press, 1978; "Family At The Beach" in *Outposts*, 1974; "The Enigma Variations" in *The New Yorker*, September 15, 1962, *The New Yorker Book Of Poems*, Viking, 1969, and in *The Race With Time And The Devil*, Golden Quill Press, 1965, in which also appeared "After The Expulsion"; "The Peaceable Kingdom" in *Epoch*, Winter, 1964; and "Orpheus" in *Confessions Of A Non-Conformist*, Hillside Press, 1963.

Library of Congress Catalog Card Number 84-50796

ISBN: HC 0-930954-21-1 PB 0-930954-22-X

FIRST EDITION

THE TIDAL PRESS

CRANBERRY ISLES · MAINE · 04625

To Lisa

An Author's Note

Perhaps a brief note is in order here to prepare the reader for a kind of poetry not currently in vogue. I call these poems "songs," a term not completely accurate in a technical sense but which conveys the musical quality aimed at. Many of these pieces use meter and rhyme and are pitched at a tone of voice more appropriate to singing than to conversation. These techniques are not popular at the moment, and the results will strike some ears as odd, archaic, irrelevant, or all three. However, I did not write these poems as a polemic. (Though I happen to believe that recent poetry has placed too much emphasis on the image and too little on sound, I have no quarrel with "free" verse, have written it all my life and will continue to write it long after the pendulum, now visibly turning, has entered its backward swing.) I wrote these poems because I love songs—the way they echo in the ear, repeat themselves over and over in the mind when you are in your shower, waiting for a bus or lying in bed at night before going to sleep. My one worry is not the suitability of the genre to the age, but the worthiness of these particular poems to their kind.

Contents

Strange Gravity

Strange Gravity

Strange gravity—that, as I grow
downwards, towards the earth,
loosens those fingers, one by one,
that bound me from my birth.

Attractions of light diminish, birds
sing in ambiguous keys.
Red flowers close. The moon sinks down
behind black-netted trees.

What but some huger, darker planet
swimming out of the night
could break this ancient spell and wean me
from this green world of light?

After the Expulsion

Light as a figment of belief
the garden left their memories.
The world outside seemed formed to please,
and there were anodynes for grief.

At first, in strange, incendiary skies,
they watched the sun give up its heat,
and felt beneath their naked feet
the grass blades shrivel up and die,

and in the woman's swelling girth
the dream of death approach, the snake,
and afterwards the threatened ache
of loss covering the entire earth.

But year stalked year, and summer's leaves
still wore their faultless summer hues,
in spite of autumn's colored ruse
and the white coat that winter weaves.

The light-winged ones had fled, but fled
just one tree over, perched and sung,
and over the sheer-faced hill still hung
that lucid disc, that matchless head.

And then the quarrel—outrage—cries—
and blood to water the desert's root.
And they remembered the garden's fruit,
and which green side was Paradise.

Bell Song

Into the mouths of bells
we vanish, one by one.
The hours toll the faces
into oblivion.

Like snuffed out candles winking
into the great, blue dark
we disappear, we vanish,
leaving behind no mark.

Except for the echoes rising
out of the mouths of bells,
making the dense air tremble
with their long farewells.

Then let those great bronze clappers
beat on their metal hides
and send the echoes pulsing
over the countryside.

Mourn! mourn for us all, you hours
that mark the time of day,
and in your bronze-tongued mourning
wear the world away.

Shabby with Fog the Woods Perspire

Shabby with fog, the woods perspire.
Disgruntled houses rise like old
abandoned hulks. The grey church spire
trickles up and disappears.

Birds in the boughs squat, mesmerized
by the endless fallings of the rain,
seeping from leaf to soggy leaf.
A cat limps through the sodden weeds.

Grey-ridden world, lost in your mind's
dyspeptic dreams and imaginings,
I feel the dull drip drip of time,
the slow, damp rottings of my life.

The Peaceable Kingdom

In separate cages, oh my Love,
we keep our striped identities
and celebrate across cool bars
our sensual amenities.

We know the tricks of claws, and know
how cages brighten lovers' charms,
but in our dreams how all worlds lie
tiger to tiger in our arms.

Song in the Face of Endings

Dearest, when I can see
the end of you-and-me—
the dark tears swelling out like buds
on the tree of ecstasy—

and think how all things waste,
how nothing we love can last,
how even the very rocks and stones
hurry into the past—

what is there to do but stare
into the blank-faced air,
and with an unbelieving mind
and feelings madness swear

that what I know's a lie—
that this being you-and-I,
once having bloomed upon love's blackening tree,
shall always be.

The Bridge

What is it now, that once the lights
glided beneath the bridge and on,
yet stayed like tethered moons and shone
on two bent faces framed by night.

All memories are the river's own.
Tonight those lamps still hang, yet seem
hurtled beyond the bend of dreams,
and of two faces one is gone.

Vivid as Windows Reflecting Moonlit Waters

Vivid as windows reflecting moonlit waters
your face shines out,
caught in the strange, dark looking glass of dreams.

But back comes the day. The mirror clouds,
the waters turn opaque—
the windows empty of all that dazzling light.

Orpheus

And where her shadow was, was sun—
And fear had lost what song had won.
By love consumed, by doubt deceived,
he turned—to air, and he believed.
That lyre was helpless now which wet
the Furies' cheeks with tears of jet;
and second knocks on Hades' door
made all that monster's dog-heads roar.
He turned again, and found that land
where Faith forgets her either hand;
where Time (by love) tears limb from limb
those lovers who would halter him;
and Pain alone has songs to save
the singer from the living grave.

The Pause

The crow sits on a jutting stone
above a field of snow—
one black, heroic period
in a world of flow.

Then flaps his wings and lumbers
into the air, to fly—
one small, black dot dissolving
in an endless sky.

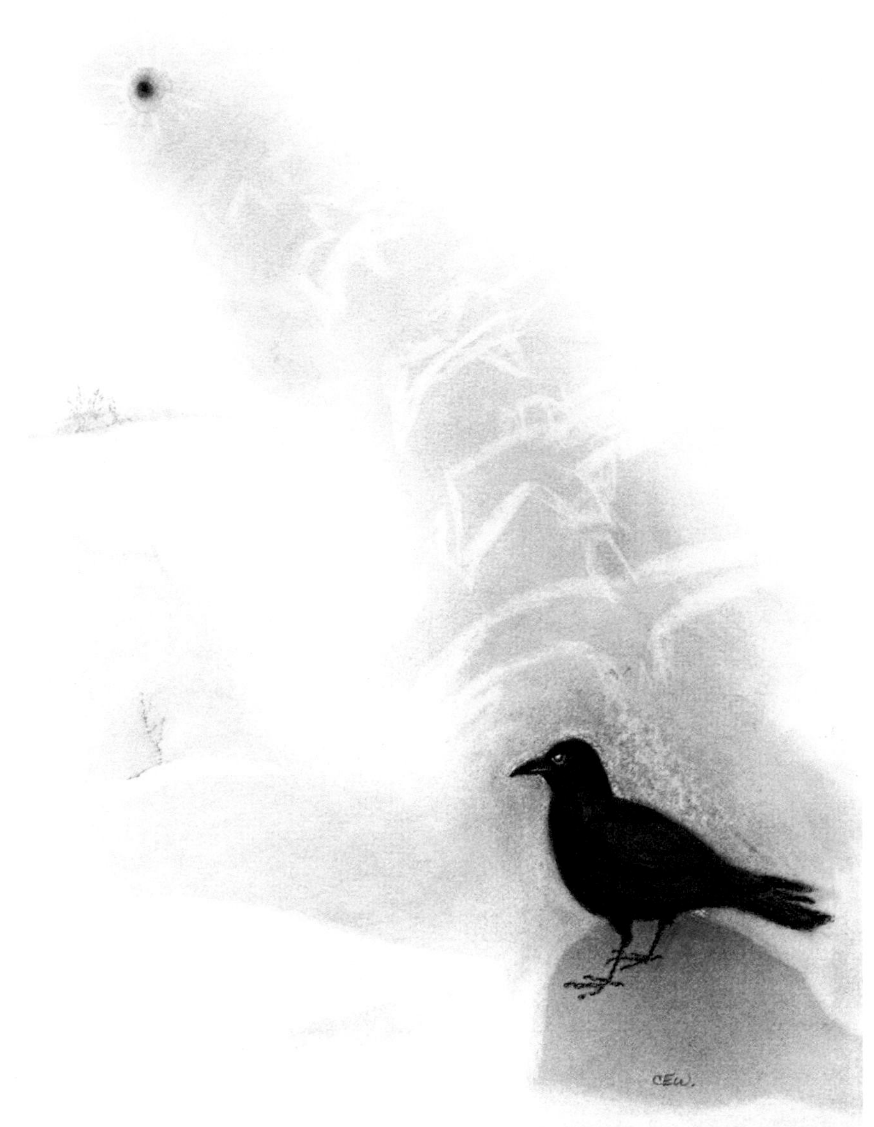
CEW.

Song of the Two Ways

Some, seizing the good time, love
as dreams and the body move,
economists of joy
who let no sun pass by
unsavored to the full,
though the long shadows fall,
and friends like streetlights pass
in parades of loneliness.

And some, suspecting green,
live by the ways of stone,
keeping whatever ends
fast-mortared in the hands
of the will (though Time's shadow
battens among the dead),
and live in a longed-for world
they cannot touch or hold.

The Death of Birds

Because the trees are seldom
bare—even in dead winter—
and others answer roll
in the morning ranks of song,
they slip away, unseen.

There is something sinister
in the way they go—unwitnessed,
falling covertly down
into the deep-strewn leaves
with the soft thud of raindrops,
the floor of the forest littered
with invisible graves;

no stone to mark their place,
no wound in earth, but flowers
blooming for the sake of flowers,
and in the boughs, still warm
with departed lives, birds
singing no requiem.

The Descent

For Freddie,
dead of leukemia at 16 years

The sparrow struck the glass and fell,
fluttered its wings, then dazed lay still.
From its tall circles in the sky
the hawk saw all, with piercing eye,
stooped, and in a whistling rush
bent down the boughs of an alder bush—
then gliding in, too swift for sight,
cleansed the earth of that small weight.

For thirteen years in that ringed eye
you lived—in misery, hope and joy.
Tardy marauder! Courageous heart
to brave so long the stoop of dark.
Now one brief rush and earth lies bare
of all that courage, suffering, fear.
And we, left kneeling on this bare ground,
wonder—at what was lost—and found.

The Moving Deep

Nothing is done that is not forgotten.
Open your eyes and let them flow.
Each tear that drops is a stone fallen
from the stairs of sorrow.

The heart aching is the heart mending,
and heart-broken is a new birth.
The rising and the falling have no ending
even under the earth.

White wings, unfurled, snare the sunlight—
then darkness on the wings of the dove;
so the shadow falls struck in the night
by darkness above.

There is no dam in the ethereal river.
Narcissus could not bear that glass—
the dropping image cracks the mirror
and present time endures its past.

Then bow your head—shoot your arrows,
tears, into the moving deep.
Lay down the bow and search the ocean—
no shafts, an empty quiver. Weep!

The Flight

Swallows front the dying sun.
They perch in rows upon black wires
watching that orange disc drop down,
breasts flushed with his gold afterfires.

Weeks of soft, aching dusks they're there,
strung out like beads in silent rows,
and then, one dusk, the wires are bare—
and they've gone—wherever summer goes.

Reciprocal

The clouds drift by—
inside my head—behind my eye—
white thoughts, drifting, over an inner sky.

And I also,
like some white cloud of feathery snow,
over the curved, blue heavens—drifting—go.

Someone is Running Away

Someone is running away.

Their feet leave marks on the moon
the size of seas.

In the branches of a hawthorn tree,
a blackbird's eating the berries.
His beak thrusts in. Red juice
runs down the face of night.

Immured in this body,
I am thinking sad thoughts about age
and the slow devourings of love.

The moon slips under a cloud.
The wind is shifting the dense, black shadows
of trees.

In the branches of a white hawthorn,
a blackbird's eating the berries.
His beak jabs in and out. The taut flesh
sighs.

There is no moon in the sky.
The wind is moving the thick, black shadows
of trees.

Someone is running away.

In the Meridian of Night

As the deeply-tired body
moves through the rooms of sleep,
tracing with vacant fingers
the worn table's top,
and gliding along the window's
cold-starred length of night,
like a left child the heart
gathers from dark corners
the echoes of old sounds,
and shadow forms that flit
over dim walls and melt,
and feels upon the grate
the warm-remembered flames.

The Room

Do not look in the room! The blinds are deeply drawn;
the door is locked; the walls are stone;
and though the roof has fallen to the bone,
and deeper, do not look in the room.
Respect the haunted now that the ghost has flown.
Respect the right of defeat to be alone,
now the gift is given and that is gone
which is not ever given. Do not look in the room.
The ceremony of justice has been said;
time given back that sun which was its own.
The book of truth has been completely read;
mourners paid for the tears which they have shed;
the preacher for his words; the wound for what it bled;
now all those gallant angels may go home.
Remember how the heart must put to bed
its hungry children. Do not look in the room.
Respect the right of death to count its dead,
and shame its failures. Do not look in the room!

Rebuttal

Once I had all the answers
to prove this strange life good—
to justify God's ways to man,
man's ways to God—
and lived in an abstract ecstasy
of brotherhood.

Grown old, now all those answers,
like wax in a candle's flame,
dribble into an endless void
of grief and pain,
and back come all the questions
from which the answers came.

The Enigma Variations

Lying in the dark music,
thinking of faceless friends,
or those kept whole but marred
by envy or turned self-hate,
and Father's upturned face
fishing the lily ponds
of pain, alone, the moon
bandaging his head,
and all good children grown
up to the four winds,
tears move upon my face
like half notes on a sheet,
and I would be a grave
walked on by stones to keep
even a mouldering faith,
though time is the heart of music.

The Widow's Night Song

Let the window close,
let the blinds come down,
let the hunched moon stare—
though all night love
look up, squint-eyed,
at an unlit square—
till the night goes,
till the stars drown.

I have places to leave—
I have things to undo—
The fabric of hands
can rip, like moth-
riddled cloth, to shreds,
and the heart's demands,
beyond conceiving,
mix the false and true.

This white pillow holds
nothing but dreams—
brief, bodiless lies,
and this slant hollow
loneliness
without disguise—
and a darkness cold
as forgotten names.

Dying Vision of the Dollhouse Maker

And the room shrank to a matchbox—
the bed turned small,
the lamplight dwindled until it seemed
no light at all—

and each of those tiny faces
hovering overhead,
dropping their small, enchanted pearls
upon the bed

seemed infinitely far-off, fragile
as dollhouse things—
lost in their little griefs, their hopes
and sufferings.

Absurd, in a house of make-believe,
to shed real tears—
over such minute tragedies—
such imagined fears.

Song of the Old One

As silence brings to the witness sounds
too subtle for the active ear—
dim furnace sounds, the sounds of lamps,
vibrations on the quiet air—

so loneliness, like some opened door,
admits the echoes of the past—
echoes of those once loved, long gone—
the conversations of the lost.

Sounds of your own dead selves, the sounds
of children growing beyond the walls,
night's flittery sounds, the sounds of feet
tiptoeing down dark, silent halls.

Until this present time, its sounds,
seem but intruders in the ear,
drowning with harsh, persistent noise
those vagrant tones we long to hear;

and that strict darkness, shunned so long,
appears a refuge, where each word
spoken in that loved past still sounds
in perfect stillness, clearly heard.

Song of the Condemned Witch

Having chosen the way of darkness
in contempt of light,
shall I shrink from these lithe flickerings
that shall bring me night?

Though, untaught, the body winces
at the touch of fire,
there, in that fiery heart, I'll find
my heart's desire.

And you, all you daylight people
who are burning here
that dark core of your inner souls
you love and fear,

see me vanish—change into nothing
before your eyes,
and into your mind's worst nightmares,
black-coiling, rise.

Stone Song

Stone outside,
stone within,
surrounded by
a rigid skin,

I keep safe
inside my heart
the ancient secrets
of the dark.

Like earth and fire,
all things burn,
and into other
substance turn.

Like wind and water,
all things flow—
I sit still
and watch them go.

White moon above,
like me a stone,
afloat in your endless
dark alone,

reach down and touch
this sleepless head—
with those cold fires
that warm the dead.

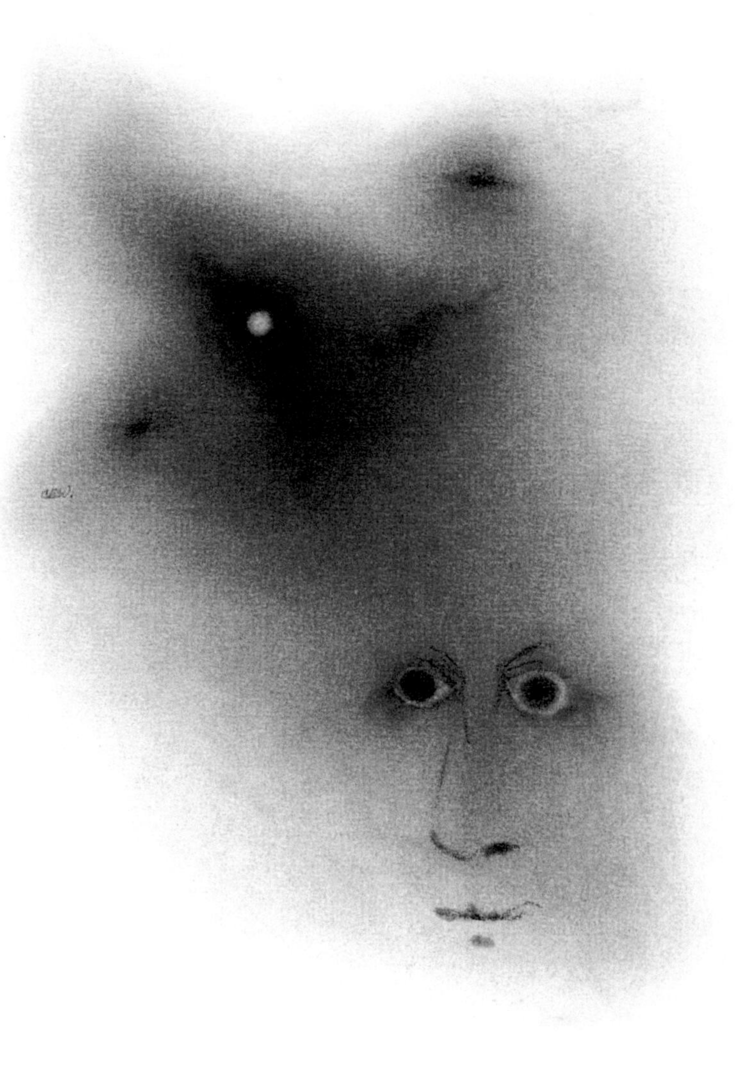

Beauty and the Beast

Dear Beast, your beastliness melts down
the marrow of my bones.
Such passion and such poverty
could melt a heart of stone.

Then in my arms transformed, a Prince,
what drove my body wild
lies beautiful, lies innocent
as a sleeping child.

But turned away in dreams, once more
that darkly pillowed head
becomes a strange, a savage thing—
alone, uncomforted.

After Finding a Spider Building a Nest in Her Hair

Grown old—but not so old as that!
Spider, what do you think you're at?—
Building a nest within my hair
to shame the grey that time set there,
presumptuous as Arachne still,
braving the gods with your small will.

Believe it or not, once I could catch
spoils of my own in this grey net,
and by a fine-spun, magic art
snare in gold strands the human heart;
but moon by month, and time by tide,
the strands loosened, the magic died.

Now caught in a web more finely spun
by a greater spinner, I lie among
old trophies, wondering at the strength
of each thin thread—its girth, its length—
and with a light hand brush you down.
Go weave in the dark your silver crown.

Song of Judas in Heaven

Condemned to Paradise,
I walk these glittering streets,
scorched by the love in every face
my face must meet.

Crying for mercy mocked,
for justice scorned, undone,
while down my cheeks the tears of grief
and mercy run.

To prove my God a man,
whom once I thought a king
I died, and through these streets his voice
comes echoing:

"Dark shadow of the sun,
sweet, necessary shade—"
and once more, by love's subtle wiles,
I am betrayed.

And pride become mere folly,
reason and honor gone,
I wander here in hopeless joy,
the fool of song;

And only when I remember
look back on earth and see
betrayer and betrayed still hanging
from the one dark tree.

The Cancer Patient to Her Dead Husband

For M.B. & R.B.

For three long years I have practiced the art of dying.
In one month, you are dead.
Quick march, like the soldier you were, scouting enemy country,
you have stolen ahead.

You who were my stay through those slow, blank midnights
when the suffering grew too much,
and only your pain in my pain gave me courage to bear it,
the strength of your touch.

Was it my long dying that wore you from the land of the living,
or just some foolish jest
that after all these years of mourning me, my going,
you should go first?

Sheer strength of will held the sun, hours past its setting,
on the rim of the fiery sky.
From too much love of the light I could not let him
drop down and die.

Now tutored by your swift passing I can see him tumble
into his cold, grey bed
unmoved, the daylight so much less lovely, more lovely
    the darkness
now you are dead.

Child's City Song

Buildings falling downwards
into your upward eyes.
Canyoned walls of windows
half blocking out the skies.

People flowing in rivers
up and down the street,
past mannequins in shop windows
that reflect their passing feet.

The policeman blows his whistle.
Metallic monsters roar.
Across the gap two armies
of moving people pour.

Balloonmen on the corner.
Ice-cream men, men with toys
that march over the counter
and back with a whirring noise.

And far-off, on the river,
the distant, magic sound
of freighters' horns saluting
the lands to which they're bound.

Child's Dream Song

Out of the upstairs window
I step upon the air
and walk across the tops of trees
without a care.

Birds in their leafy cages
suspend their whistlings
to see this strange bird walking by
without its wings.

And people and cars far under
stop in their mazy ways,
craning their necks straight upwards
and stare, amazed.

Over the gull-winged towers,
over bunched hills I go,
strolling across the backs of clouds
like drifts of snow.

Then passing the last horizon,
I turn and walk back home,
step in through my bedroom window
back to my own room.

Scarecrow's Song

Blackbird on my shoulder,
pecking out my brains,
whatever you think you're stealing, blackbird 's
not worth your pains.

Wind blows down my collar.
Rain soaks through my clothes.
I flap my arms at the windy weather
whenever the wind blows.

Sun, they say can harm you.
Sunlight can strike you blind.
I stare into the sun all day
and never lose my mind.

Or, yanked from my perch by children,
in the bending weeds I lie
watching the white clouds chase the grey clouds
over the summer's sky.

Take nothing away from nothing
still nothing's left behind.
Let the rain fall down forever.
Let the wind blow the wind blind.

Though mildew eat my body,
moon shadows steal my soul,
still on the air see this ghostly scarecrow
flapping on an empty pole.

Song of the Falling Leaves

To slip—let go—drift down
through the many-leveled air,
swaying in the wind's light currents
here and there—

and falling among curled-up leaves,
veined hands that have all let go,
to lie on the crisp earth gently
as flakes of snow—

or seized by a gust of wind
to arise in swirls of rain
and go skittering over lawn and pavement
without pain.

Suspended from their stems of fire,
the stars still hang in the sky,
longing—to let go—drift down—lightly
and in darkness lie.

Song of Oedipus at Colonus

Half-seeing done, I sit
in the garden of the Gods,
surrounded by these stony
effigies.

Forgiven, all the past—
blind hate, blind love, blind pride—
and even Fate's blind, fathomless
decrees.

Warmly the slanting sun
falls upon withered hands—
on withered feet, blue shadows
lengthening—

And in the gathering dusk,
like nightingales, the Gods
open their stony throats,
and begin to sing.

Always the Hilltops Take Me

Always the hilltops take me,
and always I go—
over the slight green rise at the end of fields,
over ridges of blue
distance—and on—where to—none know.

Having lived more than half of my lifetime,
long ago I found
how hilltop leads on to hilltop, how mountain
to mountain gives ground,
past the horizon's bound.

And yet these exultant promises
still leap in my blood,
as I stand here gazing at the far blue heads of hills,
lost in the flood
of longing—for some unknown good.

O skyward leaping hungers,
you are not lies.
Though your heights give way to other hilltops rising
beyond the reach of our eyes,
you are your own eternities.

I shall rest in you—both moving
and planted here,
in these green, curving flanks, these waves of earth and stone
that cresting in air
plunge down and break—upon what far-off shore?

Repetitive Song in Springtime

"It will all go on,"
said the bird,
"when you and I are gone,"
said the bird—
"when black-barked, red-tipped trees
bear no more leaves,
and shoots,
green-bursting, rocket-speared,
yellow at the roots,
and our daily fire, the sun,"
said the bird,
"dips his face into night and is done,
and the Pleides, Orion,
the Great and the Lesser Bear
run over the sky's edge
and disappear,
and the First Word,"
said the bird,
"echoes in the last silence
of the first darkness
unheard,
and everything and everyone
is no one,"
said the bird,
"is oblivion,"
said the bird,
"it will all go on."

Weather Map

Under this blue bowl, cracked by trees,
I lie in summer, at my ease.
On the weather map, great banks of storms
reach north with whitely swirling arms.

One hour away, perhaps, slant rains
are dashing out the eyes of stones,
and under a black, fragmented sky
dim, wavery creatures flutter by.

But here in this moment's cloudless blue
I live—to this moment's weather true—
though on the map the blue bowl breaks,
the air thunders, and the earth shakes.

Family at the Beach

From a cloud, or a bird's eye,
their three black wanderings
must have made the beach more bare
that sudden spring.

Blurred by the light and wind,
his shadow seemed to run
down the blue curve of the sea;
while crouched in the sun

she sorted the colored shells
and stones; and rushing at the foam
that collapsed in rings at his feet, the boy
drove ocean home.

At the white foot of noon
meeting, they saw in the sky
appear, suddenly, a flake
of light, too high

for a bird, white as a gull's
wings—then gulls, whole reams
of gulls, spontaneous generations,
all calling their names.

Summer

Once, in the kingdom of summer,
lying beneath three trees,
I watched the curled, slow-moving clouds
drift at their ease.

And watched the cloud-fringed branches
nod in the summer's air,
turning the leaves to shields of light
white-flashing there.

Wherever those clouds were going,
they were going at their own pace,
careless of days—of destinations
in some other place.

Cicadas sang in the branches.
Tree toads opened their throats.
Birds from their three green towers dropped
enchanted notes.

Behind me, an endless summer.
Ahead, long summer days—
lengthening into twilight's deep,
blue mysteries.

Once, in the kingdom of summer,
lying in the summer's grass
I watched the curled, slow-moving clouds—
that passing, never passed.

A Valedictory Song

For H.W.

Here in this box of fading scent
one love affair, transacted, lies.
Here thrift preserves what passion spent—
five years dispatched without replies.

I read the words again, that pain
might ferret meaning from the mind;
but love, inured to dark in vain,
and blessed with hindsight, still is blind.

Tears still seem the cause of grief,
and hopelessness the reason half
our pieties turned misbelief
and love became our epitaph.

Now, joy's parishioner, the dark
a place where faith and kindness last,
this maze of stars a children's park,
I have no purpose for the past.

But call you back, dead love, to pay
the burial fees of suffering,
that what is gone should briefly stay,
and faith exact a final fling.

Night Song

They burn across the harbor—
peepholes of silver light
cut in the hill's black shadow,

marking the lives of houses
whose rooms still hoard the brightness
of day, fearing the night.

With what a fine candor
they shine, what clear-eyed sight—
longing, astringent, lonely.

I do not love those faces
that behind dark walls tonight
hide, masked in their proud pretenses;

but love these naked lights
shining out so bravely, waiting
for the rich death of sunrise.

In Praise of Loneliness

Since first creation burst
out of the egg of night
and scattered across vast darkness
fragmented light,

the ache of being single
has rankled inside the bone
of every separate creature—
from star to stone.

So when at the dawn-touched window
you watch the slow light wring
out of black massive shadows
the shapes of things—

tree profiles looming baldly
out of the tangled air—
birds growing on branches—
rooftops jutting clear—

and in each light-edged being
you feel that aching cry
exult, mourn for the loneliness
that moves both earth and sky.

The Wind That Touches No One's Hands

The wind that touches no one's hands—
that bends no grass blade, stirs no leaf—
blows from the other side of grief.

Even the hearts of birds grow small
in their frozen perches in the sky,
hearing that soundless wind rush by.

And animals in their long sleep wake,
the hair on their necks bristling,
as overhead sweeps that blind wing.

From somewhere beyond the end of time
it comes—blowing nowhere into nowhere,
and whispering into Being's ear:

"Before the First Word was—before
the sun blazed, and the stars were born
I was—and shall be when they're gone.

I am no one. I am the wind!"

Under the Garden Sleeps the Sun

Under the garden sleeps the sun.
The mole burns in that fiery eye.
From the dark places, the winds blow down.

Light rots the green roots underground.
Trees shrivel up—plants, flowers die.
Under the garden sleeps the sun.

Men walk upon their heads. Someone
upturned the world. What was low is high.
From the dark places, the winds blow down.

Virtue's mocked—Violence crowned.
Nightmares breed and multiply.
(Under the garden sleeps the sun.)

Sucked into the black-holed heavens, stars drown.
The dead wake in their graves and cry.
From the dark places, the winds blow down.

Rise up, O buried Lamp! Great One,
take back your kingdom in the sky!
But under the garden sleeps the sun.
From the dark places, the winds blow down.

The Sower

After a painting by Van Gogh

Sower by the slanting tree,
sun vast halo round your head,
sowing the dark, enchanted seeds
which as they fall are harvested—

Blue daubs of field, small yellow house,
green-yellow sky, light-streaked with pinks,
and on the low horizon poised
a moon-like sun that rising sinks—

Dark body of a slanting tree
jutting across both earth and sky
like the body of some ancient king
stripped of his robes and crucified—

And you, beneath the tree, your arm
rising and falling like the sun,
sowing the seeds of light and dark—
eternity—oblivion.

Comparison of Climates

There the sail's luxurious curve
commands a blue and endless sky.
Here a stony sun beats down
to black a world that cannot die.

There dwell the rich, bronze newlyweds,
intransients at the task of joy.
The sick live here, the lame, the mad,
and those the love of Gods destroy.

This is the country of the blind
who see the world through darkening bands,
who drink the simple leaves like moths,
and cup the sunlight in their hands.

There the landscapes riot gold,
and acts of joy bind link by link
the heart to perfect happiness.
Time is given here to think.

The body here is burned, to light
greater worlds of lesser day.
There the flesh becomes the soul
and ripens in the soul's decay.

Apples bend those amber boughs.
Here, the trees have night to give.
Eagles dive on burning wings.
In this country I would live.

When Jesus Left the Tomb

When Jesus left the tomb
he felt beneath bare feet
the glowing stones, first-touched with morning's
tender heat—

And felt the sunlight mounting,
pressing against cold flesh
to thaw from dark imprisoned bones
the chill of death—

And heard the birds of morning
pour in his wakening ear
celebrations of the sun, new-risen
from darkness' bier—

And for the first time knew
the ground on which he stood—
adjunct of Paradise, lost Eden's
hidden wood—

And saw bright spirits dancing
lightly through the body's dress,
moving from joy, to pain, to joy,
blessed and unblessed—

And dropping upon his knees
he hugged that secret earth—
the world beneath this once-born world
of death and birth.

On the Stroke of Midnight

Midnight crumbles, and the clock
sweeps with greenly glowing hands
the velvet rubble of the dark
backwards—into vanished lands.

And new-made darkness melts the chairs,
lamps, tables, sofa into strange
imaginary shapes that flow
into the shadow-shapes of change.

And into the mind past midnights pour,
and midnights unborn, yet to be,
crowding the room with formless forms,
and timeless times eternity.

While far above the roof the stars
shine in a vast and crumbling night,
sending live pictures from the past
into a present future light.

How good to join the flow, to melt
in this dark whirlpool circling down
into the present moment's still
and future silence, past and gone.

Anti-Nihilist's Song

Not nothingness, but meanings—
multiplicity of clues—
signposts pointing off like trees,
all ways to choose.

Dread, misery, despair—
felicity, delight—
whether you exult in the way-rich dark,
or fear the night.

As points on a globe swell down
in lines across its face
to meet again on the other side
in the one place,

perhaps these diverse meanings
lead back to the one end—
as strands in a spider's web lead back
to the spider's den,

or as fierce stars exploding
out of one central sun
spread out in spiral rings, then shrink
again to one.

CEW.

Death, Dark Shadow, Walk

Death, dark shadow, walk
always by my side.
In your clear shade all living things
are purified.

Gold-rich, the moving sun—
Quick-green, the gliding trees—
As swift as jewels the birds that dart
among the leaves—

And every face that passes,
haloed by that dark light,
shines out with a rich, dissolving shine
like lamps at night—

And body, poor compendium
of curious aches and pains,
takes on a grace, like weathered stone
washed by the rains.

Greed, envy, hatred, lust
melt in that scrutiny,
and the good shines clear, as in the light
of eternity.

Stay near me, guardian shadow.
Be that winged one heaven sends—
until the night falls, and in that darkness
all darkness ends.

Biographical Notes

Paul Petrie was born in Detroit, Michigan, on the outer fringes of the city. His earliest ambition to be a second baseman was succeeded, at the age of fourteen, by his decision to write the great American novel. However, at Wayne State University, where he took his B.A. and M.A., he was converted to poetry by his creative writing instructor, Richard Werry. After two dubious years in the Army, supposedly in Intelligence, he went to the State University of Iowa from which he received his Ph.D. While there he studied with Robert Lowell, John Berryman and Paul Engle at the Iowa Workshop.

Since 1959 he has taught at the University of Rhode Island, specializing in English Romantic Poetry and Creative Writing. Six collections of his poetry have been published and two hundred and seventy-nine individual poems have appeared in a variety of magazines. He is married to the printmaker, Sylvia Spencer Petrie. They have three children, Philip, Emily and Lisa.

Charles E. Wadsworth, a painter and printmaker, lives half of each year on an island off the Maine coast and the other half in the small, coastal city of Portsmouth, New Hampshire. He and his wife Jeannie, a painter and writer, have also lived in Boston and its environs and have been frequent visitors to East Dean, a tiny English village in Sussex. Their two children, Laurie and Geoffrey, are both musicians.

Mr. Wadsworth's prints, monotypes and drawings have appeared in a number of books including *Root and Sky* and *Death Is A Kind Of Love* by the British playwright Christopher Fry; *Islands Off Maine* by the Welsh poet and short-story writer Leslie Norris; *Andrew Young: Remembrance and Homage* (a memorial tribute by a number of poets to a distinguished Anglo-Scottish poet and clergyman); *Seed Leaves* by Richard Wilbur; *Fireweed and Other Poems* by William H. Matchett; *The Long Sought Landscape* by Charles Seymour Alden; and two collections of his own poetry called *Views From The Island* and *A Tourist In Ludlow*.

✲

Six
hundred
copies of this
book, three hundred
casebound and three hundred
softbound, have been printed letterpress
in Monotype Centaur and Arrighi,
on Mohawk Superfine Text
by The Stinehour Press.
Charles E. Wadsworth
and Freeman Keith
designed the
book.
The
drawings
were reproduced
photo-offset
by Meriden
Gravure.

✲ ✲
✲